Copyright © 2014 Wendy K. Walters

SELLING WITHOUT SLEAZE
MARKETING WITH A CONSCIENCE

Photos of Wendy by John Jay | johnjay1000@gmail.com

Printed in the USA

ISBN: 978-0-9862033-9-8

All Rights Reserved. This book is protected by the copyright laws of the United States of America. This book may not be copied or reprinted for commercial gain or profit. The use of short quotations is permitted. Permission will be granted upon request. The author guarantees all contents are original and do not infringe upon the legal rights of any other person or work.

Prepared for Publication By

PALM TREE
PUBLICATIONS

Palm Tree Publications is a Division of Palm Tree Productions
www.palmtreeproductions.com
PO BOX 122 | KELLER, TX | 76244

Scripture references appear in the endnotes:

Unless otherwise noted, all scripture was taken from the New King James Version (NKJV) of the Bible. Copyright © 1982 by Thomas Nelson, Inc. Used by permission. All rights reserved.

To Contact the Author:

www.wendykwalters.com

Wendy K. Walters

Live on Purpose

Dedicated to all men and women
of integrity who have something
worthwhile to share.

CONTENTS

7   CHAPTER ONE
    SICK OF SLICK

17 CHAPTER TWO
    PERSUASION VS. MANIPULATION

29 CHAPTER THREE
    MARKETING 101

59 CHAPTER FOUR
    THE BIGGER PICTURE

65 APPENDIX
    RESOURCES

MARKETING SHOULD NOT BE
ABOUT GOOD STORYTELLING.
MARKETING SHOULD BE ABOUT TELLING
A GOOD STORY WELL.

—WENDY K. WALTERS

CHAPTER ONE

SICK OF SLICK

The world is full of pushy salesmen. Charlatans. Hucksters. People who prey on anyone vulnerable to their pitch, dedicated to inflating the image of their own importance. People willing to sacrifice their first love (and perhaps their firstborn) for the possibility of notoriety and the lure of easy money.

They're slick. Oily really, and not from any measure of anointing. They may have been shallow from the start, or they might have begun with pure motives and become twisted along the way. Whatever the case, by hanging the word "Christian" after their name and in front of their product, they have given the Body of Christ a bad name. Wolves in sheep's clothing, they have flooded the market with shiny packages and programs and if you listen closely, you can't quite tell if they are offering you keys to the Kingdom or to a Mercedes Benz (in fact they seem interchangeable).

I'm a branding expert. I make my living helping people market their minds—turn their ideas into money. I create resource streams to support their mission, make possible their vision, and help them broaden their influence. I challenge others to make their mark on the world intentionally. I routinely encounter men and women of stature who genuinely have something worthwhile to offer to a hurting, hopeless world. They have unique stories and experiences, expertise in everything imaginable. They have real solutions for real problems faced by real people. Their hearts are committed to the Lord and they desire to walk worthy of their calling. Some are just discovering their true identity after years of ministry, or with a whole career behind them. They are grappling with how to articulate this new thing God is trying to do through them. Others I encounter have great clarity about their core message, but have only just begun to see the value of creating resources—products or processes that will benefit others and help them grow.

Here is what I notice: the people who have the best stuff to share shy away from packaging it and making it available to the world. They are hesitant about creating something and charging money for what they have created. Why? Because they are sick of slick. They are so desperately disgusted with that brand of modern day money-vangelist they would rather remain hidden in their tiny corner of the church. They will work passionately to impact the world one person at a time, made possible through the generous donations of others. They might not touch as many lives this way, but at least their integrity will remain intact.

Growing up I was taught, "the love of money is the root of all evil."[1] Money itself was not evil, but the love of money was certainly evil. In the back of my mind, if I did something for money, then my motives were somehow linked to the *love* of money ... and therefore, evil. I lived in a world that functioned on money, so it was a necessary evil, but evil nonetheless.

I knew it was okay to work a job you didn't like because you had to earn money, that was honest. If you owned a store or a plumbing business, that was okay too as long as you weren't *too* successful and therefore a cheat (demonstrating that the love of money was the root of your profitability). I was also taught it was good if you gave away a lot of money, although it wasn't clear to me how you could give a lot of money if you weren't allowed to earn a lot of money without being evil. (If you were evil, you probably wouldn't be giving your money away in the first place, right?)

Certainly *everything* that could be categorized as "ministry" ought to be done for free ... and just about everything that brought benefit, blessing, or enjoyment to another person was tucked firmly under the "ministry" category in my mind. The bottom line revealed I was programmed to believe if I did anything I really, *really* enjoyed and charged money for it, there was something not quite wholesome about my motives.

Explained like that, it feels ridiculous. But I had never actually spelled out my belief system about money. I didn't think about what I thought. I just lived with a worldview that gave me a relationship with money that was cynical at best and hostile at worst. I hovered somewhere between the poverty gospel (that truly righteous people don't care about money, and therefore have very little of it to worry about) and the prosperity gospel (that righteous people live blessed and that blessing is evident by having lots of nice things bought with the money which demonstrated how blessed they were). I landed firmly in the middle and felt guilty about everything all the time.

Even opportunities to expand my influence or share my voice sent me into a tailspin of questioning the purity of motives. I honestly wanted to walk worthy of my calling and steer clear of anyone or anything that might disqualify

SICK OF SLICK

my service to the King. It was my desire to live right that in many cases kept me from living at all. In fact, I once considered cancelling a major speaking engagement after I learned the names of some others who would also appear on the program. I was terrified I would be guilty by association. If I showed up where they were, people might think I was just like them. I so much didn't want to be "THAT" that I was ready to not be anything. I can almost see you nodding your head in agreement. Maybe you too have shrunk back from yourself because you didn't like the look of others who were operating in a similar space. Maybe like me you are turned off by "THAT," so it seems better to seal off your borders, "come out from among them and be ye separate."[2]

Then I realized this was exactly the enemy's strategy. In order to keep me from showing up and accomplishing my assignment, he had convinced me that shrinking back from opportunity and retreating to what felt like moral high ground was the righteous thing to do.

With the purest of motives, I was giving people I wasn't even in relationship with a measure of control in my life. I had seen enough sleaze and salesmanship passed off under the banner of Christianity to turn me off forever. It felt better to go back into my prayer closet. Safer at least. There in fellowship with Jesus I could walk in the cool of the day and be content.

SELLING WITHOUT SLEAZE

But I wasn't.

My city was supposed to sit on a hill.[3] I was supposed to be as a sheep in the midst of wolves, wise as a serpent and as harmless as a dove.[4] I was supposed to let my light so shine before men that they would see my good works and glorify my Father in heaven. That was pretty hard to do from my closet.

FILL YOUR SPACE

"Fill your space," I heard.

"What does that mean?" I asked.

"Fill your space. Don't puff yourself up to try to look like something larger than I have made you, and don't shrink back from anything I have called you to be. Just fill your space," He answered.

A light went on in my heart.

How dare I not show up? How dare I remain sealed off from the world, hiding. God wanted me to show up fully clothed in the identity He wrapped me in, operating in the authority He gave me, to complete the work He sent me to do!

That was the last time I struggled with this. Now when I encounter it in others, a fiery passion comes over me to

SICK OF SLICK

expose this lie. Maybe you will recognize it in one of these familiar scenarios:

- The pastor of a small church feels uncomfortable about marketing. "Isn't Jesus enough?" He asks me, "What we have here is so good, I can't understand why we aren't reaching more people. We shouldn't need to advertise."

- The godly woman overflowing with priceless experience is hesitant to write her book because she isn't looking for fame or recognition. Truly, she doesn't care about that. It feels uncomfortable to her to declare to the world that she has a message worth reading, that feels self-serving. She can just hear them, "Who does she think she is, anyway?"

- The fledgling Christian entrepreneur has just started a business and was told that if their business was truly a God-thing, God would bring in the customers for them. Marketing demonstrates a lack of faith. (Seriously, I've heard this one!)

- The silver-haired man of God is filled with wisdom and burning with revelation and insight. "I don't understand facebook," he tells me, "I just don't get it. I am not looking for my fifteen seconds of fame. I care about substance. There is just too much foolishness on social media."

- "I have a ministry planning weddings ... (or helping people lose weight, or creating a financial plan, or adjusting their priorities to meet life goals, or decorating a home on a budget, or cooking healthy, or preparing for a job interview, or passing a nursing exam ... insert your passion here). It doesn't feel right to charge money for that. I just like to help people."

- Or how about this one: "People tell me all the time I should write a book, but I figure enough books have already been written on this subject, why does the world need one more?"

Let me tell you why. The world needs to hear from you precisely because you have something worthwhile to say. The world needs to see you precisely because your heart's desire is to serve One who is greater, and we haven't seen nearly enough of those kind of people. The world needs you to start a business out of the things you are naturally gifted to do and you need to understand, "In all hard work there is profit, but endless talking about it only brings poverty."[5] Yes, social media *is* filled with foolishness and the world needs a little substance to make an appearance.

Entrepreneurs need to market their business ... as do ministries and churches. Christians have the harmless as doves part down in spades, but the wise as serpents part has been totally overlooked! It is possible to market yourself and remain qualified to ascend into the hill of the Lord with clean hands and a pure heart—a soul not lifted up to falsehood or deceitfulness.[6]

I hope this little book will put your mind at ease about packaging what you have and offering it to the world. True branding is simply coming into agreement with your God-given identity and making sure the package you wrap it in is congruent with the contents. A diamond ring ought to be in a beautiful velvet box, not wrapped in a greasy paper bag, don't you think? If you are looking for a diamond ring, which package would attract you?

Let's take a look at why marketing seems to repulse people with a conscience. Let's find out why they struggle to boldly declare who they are and place a monetary value on their worth.

ENDNOTES:

1. 1 Timothy 6:10.
2. 2 Corinthians 6:17.
3. Matthew 5:14.
4. Matthew 10:16.
5. Proverbs 14:23, NET Bible.
6. Psalm 24:3-5.

SELLING WITHOUT SLEAZE

CHAPTER TWO

PERSUASION VS. MANIPULATION

Marketing is necessary to every business. Every organization that needs to interact with people to communicate a message and invite participation of any kind needs to market itself. Marketing isn't evil, it is integral. In *Marketing Your Mind,* I communicate how we market ourselves every day, whether we have anything to sell or not. Transactions are not limited to the exchange of money.

Leaders must create "buy in" for their vision. Parents are trying desperately to create "buy in" with their children to adopt their moral code as their own, to live according to a values system, and develop godly character. Any time you require a transaction—including agreement with an idea or obedience to a directive—you have successfully marketed your mind. Chances are you do this naturally through persuasion and exercising your influence. You do it without thinking.

Winning someone over to your point of view, unlocking a revelation or truth, opening a mind … these are all things you love to do. A surge of energy goes through you when you know you have done it well. It fuels your need to create value, in fact, to be valuable. It allows you to feel significant. It feels good to persuade someone to make a good decision, a better choice. You lead them to an idea and watch with joy when they grab it and make it their own.

If you are reading this book, chances are you already have the skills you need to present information convincingly, spell out an idea clearly, provide facts, and lead someone to make a decision. It is time to take what you do naturally with ideas and learn how to apply that to marketing yourself, your business, or your ministry.

There is a big difference between persuasion and manipulation. I don't buy into the idea that there is a fine line separating them. I think the line is thick and obvious.

PERSUASION VS. MANIPULATION

A POWERFUL, POSITIVE FORCE

Persuasion is a powerful force. Our own persuasions hold us to our moral code. They keep us grounded in our beliefs even in the midst of a contradiction. "I am fully persuaded."[1] Using persuasion allows us to influence the beliefs, choices, or behavior of others. Used the right way, persuasion is a gift from God. It helps us direct people to good things—to point them, if you will. The Holy Spirit is the ultimate persuader. He points people to Jesus, always. He never manipulates. He never tricks anyone to choose Jesus under false pretenses.

Persuasion is an art. Persuasion is used to advise or urge someone toward a choice. Persuasion appeals to reason or understanding, lays out a case in the open, and asks the listener to decide for themselves. It isn't covert or surreptitious. It is done in the daylight.

We all have some common core needs: the need to feel loved, the need to feel valuable, to feel secure, to make a difference, the need for ... for whatever! Persuasive marketing allows you to highlight a need and link it to the idea (the product, the book, the service) you are offering. This is one of the reasons it is so important to understand who your target audience is. Not only will they share common core needs, they will share them passionately. When you identify with them in these areas, your voice resonates.

Persuasion chooses words carefully, with intentionality, seeking to communicate passion, motive, and method.

When you use persuasion, you have the other person's interests in mind. You seek to leave them better than you found them. You believe in the value of what you are offering and want others to have the opportunity to experience what you know. You care about what happens AFTER a sale has been made. You want them to be better because they encountered what you have to offer. You know your name is on the line and you care about your name. You value your reputation because you have built it carefully.

THE DARK SIDE OF THE MOON

Manipulation is also an art. A dark art. Manipulation is using influence to handle someone in an unfair manner. It is a skill set developed to gain an advantage and leverage it in favor of the one doing the manipulating. Just as persuasion is not limited to marketing a product, neither is manipulation. You see it used every day, dozens of times. For many it has become second nature. They don't even know how to approach someone without twisting the approach to secure what they want, the way they want it.

PERSUASION VS. MANIPULATION

Manipulation employs tactics. It too recognizes core needs, but instead of seeking to resonate with the needs of people, it exploits them. Manipulation marketing preys on the emotions. It looks for emotional triggers and capitalizes on them. It works best when the audience is not fully aware of what they are up to. For example, manipulation will prey on someone's sense of duty and make an offer seem like the only responsible thing to do. It cashes in on someone's fear of being left out of what others have taken advantage of, and a pitch is crafted that promises status or satisfaction.

Manipulation parses words carefully seeking to distract, mislead, or adapt a situation to sway in favor of the manipulator.

Manipulation is what happens when persuasion becomes twisted. Those who use it have their own interests in mind. Their agenda is to get a person to do what they want them to do, buy what they want them to buy … at all costs. It's heady.

A rush of adrenalin comes when people want what you offer. It is validating. It gets even more exciting when they buy what you have to sell. The feeling is so intoxicating you have to protect yourself from it, or the high you feel from acceptance can trump the purpose you set out to achieve in the first place. Like the number of "likes" on a facebook status, whether or not someone signs on the bottom line can become a referendum on your self-worth. Purchase is proof of relevance, or at least of popularity.

Manipulation boils it all down to a game of averages. There is nothing wrong with averages. Understanding how they work for your business or ministry is important. But manipulating the numbers just for the sake of numbers is not about a mission (unless the mission is all about numbers and does not include the consideration of people).

It is fact that a certain percentage of people will buy at a certain price point. Not only that, but a small percentage of those people will be willing to spend a little more, and a smaller percentage of those who spent a little more will be willing to spend a lot more. A tiny percentage will also want their money back no matter what. This is the Pareto Principle, the 80/20 rule in action and it is valuable to know how it works. It can dramatically increase your efficiency and profitability, but it can easily be twisted to take advantage of people.

Manipulation delights in playing the odds. It capitalizes on emotions and leverages the undisciplined, compulsive buying habits of unsuspecting people. Those who manipulate care little about what happens AFTER a transaction has been made. Their concern is not with the quality or usefulness of their offering. Their goal is to make as many sales as possible to up the percentages, put more

PERSUASION VS. MANIPULATION

people in the pipeline, and fatten up the bottom line. If a life happens to improve in spite of that, great. If not, not my problem. "Buyer beware" is your responsibility.

Let's break down the differences between persuasion and manipulation:

PERSUASION	MANIPULATION
Powerful force to influence choices.	Powerful force to direct choices.
Appeals to reason, seeks to increase understanding.	Appeals to emotion, capitalizes on confusion.
Is overt—operates in the light.	Is covert—prefers the shadows
Resonates with common core needs of people.	Exploits the common core needs of people.
Chooses words carefully, is eloquent.	Parses words, practices "slight of tongue."
Has open, clear motives.	Has hidden, veiled motives.
Seeks to increase value and benefit others.	Seeks to benefit its own interests.

SELLING WITHOUT SLEAZE

The line between these two forces is clear. Understand, not every person who has fallen into the trap of getting people to cooperate with their agenda through manipulation has dark motives at heart. For many manipulation has been modeled as the best way to get things done. It is as effective to sign up volunteers as it is to sell widgets. Manipulation has been taught to us from the cradle. Our mothers used it to make us wear sweaters because guilt was more expedient than education. We all recoil in disgust when we recognize someone manipulating others harmfully. But if we didn't have at least some fascination with watching people shamelessly manipulate others and loving it when someone at last gets one over on them, Reality TV would soon be off the air. I wish it was limited to slick salesman, but I have seen plenty of good people with good motives use manipulation to get others behind their goals. There is a better way. Reject manipulation. Develop the art of persuasion.

THE CURRENCY OF TRUST

Trust is the currency of influence, the coin of the realm. Whether you are a parent teaching a child to ride a bicycle, a doctor prescribing medication to alleviate suffering, or a realtor selling someone their first home, trust is an asset. The one receiving from you must trust you, or you are going to have a hard time achieving a goal together.

PERSUASION VS. MANIPULATION

In marketing, establishing trust with your audience is key to having them believe your words and accept your ideas. Your non-verbal communication is as important as your spoken words. Your body language has to align with what you are saying if you are to remain convincing and credible. Any incongruence between the two sabotages your rapport and your chance for a meaningful, lasting exchange evaporates.

I have watched someone speak, communicating boldly from the platform with confidence, poise, and authority. The moment they went to talk about the resources they had available, their body language changed. They became apologetic and over-explained everything. Even the rhythm of their speech and hand gestures changed. It was clear how uncomfortable they were asking someone to purchase something. They had poured out their heart, delivered well, and the whole crowd was eating out of their hand and hungry for more, but now the whole thing suddenly felt "off." Though they spoke about their product (book, CD, DVD, coaching program, profile, whatever, …), they were communicating with their body language that they would prefer to skip this part altogether. Their discomfort devalued their resources. In trying so diligently NOT to manipulate someone, they failed to persuade anyone.

SELLING WITHOUT SLEAZE

It is hard for people to make a decision to take another step with you—engage with your book, hire you as a consultant, sign up for your coaching calls or seminar—if you look like you want to jump out of your own skin the moment you have to communicate the price of anything.

The other extreme is when a person pours it on and whatever ease they were communicating with is switched off and the hard sell turns on. No matter how genuine the message was or how clearly it resonated with the audience, a hungry used car salesman now stands before them, double-tongued and greedy for gain.[2] He is going to hold them captive until he pushes them into whatever lemon he's trying to unload. This person also devalues their resources (though they are decidedly better at gaining results than the previous example). Anything that needs this much hype—this much hard sell to convince you to buy or join or sign—probably has a catch. Some people are really good at winding up the pitch and forcing a sale. I know this because six months later I will hear, "Oh yeah, I bought all So-and-So's stuff ... I never even opened it. It is still somewhere in my garage. I have no idea why I bought it!"

A sale was made, but no meaningful transaction of life, experience, or expertise was exchanged. It didn't matter whether what was offered was needed (or even desired), it was all about making the sale. This kind of person has

PERSUASION VS. MANIPULATION

to continuously find new people to talk to because they wear thin on an audience who has heard them before. They are constantly driven to create new products. (I know, if it's a ministry we have to call them resources, of course.) This type of person has exchanged authenticity for arrogance and checked their conscience at the door along with their coat.

Neither situation pleases God. Neither example reflects a person who knows who they are and truly values what they have to offer. One shrinks back and the other puffs up. Both fall short.

When you are fully persuaded, you have no internal conflict with being persuasive. Engaging with persuasion allows you to maintain respect for your audience. You appreciate when trust has been extended and desire to maintain that trust by walking in authenticity and operating in full disclosure. You can be persuasive and remain honest and unapologetic about what you have to offer.

> **WHEN YOU ARE FULLY PERSUADED, YOU HAVE NO INTERNAL CONFLICT WITH BEING PERSUASIVE.**

You will be clear about what it costs to engage, and seek to communicate the value, the risk, and the reward. There is never a cause to be upset when someone determines they do not need or do not want what you

SELLING WITHOUT SLEAZE

offer. You understand that engaging with the right people at the right time for the right reason is rewarding and fruitful. There is no need to manipulate people in order to market effectively.

Let's take a look at what clear, honest marketing looks like.

ENDNOTES:

1. Romans 8:38-39.
2. 1 Timothy 3:8.

CHAPTER THREE

MARKETING 101

I became a student of marketing and branding years ago. The subject fascinates me and I read everything I can get my hands on about business. I study how brands are built, why colors are used, how ads are targeted, and what good copy editing looks like. Not only do I regularly increase my knowledge of business and branding, I combine what I learn with my passion for helping people step fully into their identity. I come alive when they move with intentionality toward their assignment—the work they were created to do. I view work as worship.[1]

SELLING WITHOUT SLEAZE

My transition from full-time worship pastor to branding consultant and author coach was an interesting (and somewhat bumpy) path. When I first began to charge people for consulting, my clients were mostly ministries, and my prices were a pittance. I literally battled feeling like Jesus was going to come out with a whip, flip over my table, point His finger at me at shout, "Moneychanger!"[2] It was terrifying.

Of course, that was nonsense, but it was a real hurdle for me. I had to overcome this paradigm that selling my intellectual property—my experience and expertise—somehow cheapened me. I never once had a problem paying to see or speak with my doctor, writing a check to my accountant or lawyer. I had no trouble paying a contractor, dentist, mechanic, or hair stylist. I purchased the books I read and paid tuition for the classes I took. I paid a registration fee for seminars I attended, and even had a gym membership where I paid to exercise! I paid for all of those things because I needed what the people had to offer. They had things that made my life better. Somehow, becoming the person who got paid was a stretch across a gap in my mindset that rivaled the Grand Canyon.

Let me cut through all the agony of my struggle and boil this down for you in the shortest, clearest way possible. Marketing is simply this: This is who I am. This is what I have to offer. This is what it costs. This is how you get it. Period.

MARKETING 101

> # MARKETING 101
>
> - **THIS IS WHO I AM**
> - **THIS IS WHAT I HAVE TO OFFER**
> - **THIS IS WHAT IT COSTS**
> - **THIS IS HOW YOU GET IT**

This simple, straightforward formula has served me well. Following it takes the anxiety out of selling. I am more concerned about engaging people's hearts and minds than I am their wallets. If I craft my offer well, and I truly believe in the product or service I am proposing, there is no reason for me to shrink back from my price. I have no need to twist anyone's arm, prey on emotions, or hard sell them into my program.

I don't need to trick them into buying now. I am building something sustainable. If I am interesting and engaging and creating a larger conversation, I can be completely content to let them walk away having only browsed and not bought. I don't care if they ever buy, but if they need what I have to offer, there is no reason to feel guilty about charging a fair price. It is honest business, conducted in the light of day. I have a clear conscience. I'm good at what I do. I believe in what I have created. I am excited when people want to learn what I know and put it to good use.

If you have struggled with this, then let me help you get past your mental hurdle. I am going to share a few simple marketing tools you can use to communicate what you have to offer. They are basic, straightforward, and easy to begin using today.

1. BUILD YOUR BRAND

Part One of my book, *Marketing Your Mind,* is dedicated to branding yourself. If you haven't given serious thought to the imprint of identity you are leaving behind you, I recommend you read the book and start to craft your impression on purpose.

For this book, I will limit the discussion on branding to a short list of why your brand matters and what it includes. I cannot stress enough how foundational your brand is to everything you communicate. It is the cornerstone upon which all your marketing will be built. All products or services will impact the brand and be impacted by the brand. You cannot ignore this important step. Here is why it matters:

MARKETING 101

- **Your brand allows you to maximize your originality.**

    It helps you focus on what is unique about you. I like to call it "The 2% Factor." While watching the Science Channel with my son one evening, I learned that under a microscope, the DNA of all dog breeds is remarkably similar. In fact, 98% of all DNA markers are common, whether you are studying the DNA of a Chihuahua or a Rottweiler. All of their unique distinctions—size, shape of snout, shape of ears, fur, length of legs and tail, tone of bark, etc. is derived from only 2% of their DNA. This small sampling, "The 2% Factor," is what makes them completely different from each other.

    The same holds true for us. 98% of the human experience is common to all mankind. Too much of our focus is on what makes us relate to each other, what makes us just like everyone else. Branding forces you to focus on the 2% that makes you completely different from everybody else. It's the filter through which you push the other 98% of your experiences so your voice is unique and strong. It helps you find your voice and create your signature sound.

- **Your brand is the imprint of your identity, and therefore, the foundational piece of all your marketing communication.**

SELLING WITHOUT SLEAZE

- **Your brand is the extension of your name—the basis for your reputation.**[3]

- **Your brand is a reflection of the image of God in you.** Branding gives you the freedom to walk comfortably in your identity. It brings clarity and removes the veil of confusion.[4]

- **Your brand is comprised of your Brand Promise (Core Values, Core Competencies, Mission, and Vision).**

- **Your brand is more than your logo.** Your brand elements are created from your Brand Promise and include: Your Name (or Business/Ministry Name), Logo Design, Graphic Standards, Tagline/Slogans, Messaging, and your Packaging and Presentation.

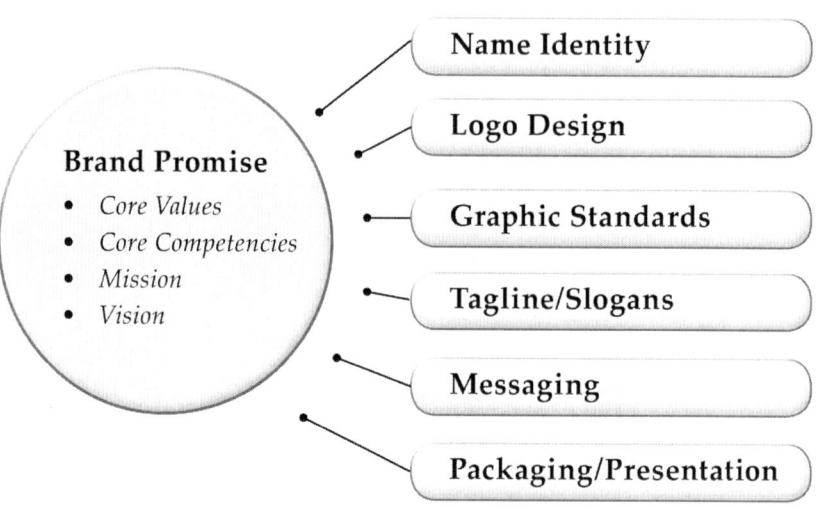

Remember our simple formula for marketing? This is who I am. This is what I have to offer. This is what it costs. This is how you get it.

Branding answers, "This is who I am." Now, what do you have to offer?

2. MASTER YOUR MESSAGE, DECLARE YOUR MASTERY

The process of branding will also help you determine your core competencies and clearly understand your mission (or assignment). Now you need to think in terms of how you can make what you have to offer deliverable to the world.

Maybe it is a book. A book is a great way to declare your expertise. It shows people how you view the world, your unique perspective. A book can demonstrate your experience with things you have mastered, obstacles you have overcome, and truth you have put into practice.

Maybe for you what you have to offer is creating a profile or a coaching/consulting process. Perhaps it is curriculum or a training course people can go through. Maybe you have created products … I don't know. Whatever it is you have to sell, you have to communicate with people what that is and how it will benefit them.

When I work with people, particularly those who are building a business built on expertise, I have them create packages that clearly outline the deliverables. People want to know what they can expect from you in exchange for money they pay you. Whether you are working in an arena you deem "sacred" or "secular," you should stand out—the best and the brightest, excelling in wisdom and knowledge.[5] Know what you are good at, know what you can consistently deliver, and be able to communicate this with people.

If you have created a product, focus on why yours is different. Why is it better? Why is it NOT like other products out there that my seem similar. Outline benefits. Boldly declare.

Assess honestly if there is a demand for your product or service? Is there an audience for your book larger than your mother and your favorite aunt? If not, call it a journal and tuck it back in your desk drawer ... then go write a different book! Are there people out there who want or need what you've got? This leads us to determining your target market.

MARKETING 101

3. TARGET YOUR MARKET

Who has the problem you solve? Are you fishing in a "Red Ocean" or have you determined where your "Blue Ocean" is located?

Picture a sea of fisherman. The waters are crowded with boats, everyone fishing in the same spot competing for the same fish. The waters are bloodied with the cut-throat competition. There is an urgency to grab what you can before someone else takes it. There is pressure. The big guys with the wide nets definitely have the advantage as the little guy's boat gets tossed about in their wake.

What if you took a little time to figure out where the water was clear and few, if any, were there to fish? What if you determined where your "Blue Ocean" of opportunity lay? In these waters, you dominate the niche. You are fishing with the right bait. The water is calm and so is the pace. It no longer matters if your boat is big or little because it's the only one out there. What if you followed God's leading and had only to cast your net over the other side of the boat and it came back too full to haul in?[6]

You do this by knowing exactly what kind of fish you are best suited to catch, where they swim, and what kind of bait they prefer. You do this by being

SELLING WITHOUT SLEAZE

unexpected. You do this by NOT duplicating everyone else's formula, even if their formula is successful for them. You don't have to re-invent the wheel, you can just innovate the wheel you've already got! Be the first if at all possible, and if you can't be the first, then create something new, something original where you can be the first.

AIM BIG, MISS BIG. AIM SMALL, MISS SMALL.

This is a saying taken from archery. Conventional wisdom says, "Aim big!" It is the shotgun approach to marketing—you're bound to hit *something*. But if you point your bow in the general direction of the big target and just let the arrow fly, you'll be lucky to hit the wall. Chances are your arrow will bounce off the target entirely and hit absolutely nothing at all.

In terms of your target market, unless you have an "As Seen on TV" product that you want to saturate an unsuspecting market with by selling once with no need for repeat customers, "Aim big," can also mean "miss big." You are better off to define your niche more carefully.

MARKETING 101

Picture a bullseye. If you take careful aim at the very center—the smallest part of the target—*then* release your arrow, chances are that even if you don't hit the bullseye, you'll be in a nearby concentric ring.

By narrowing the concentration on your target market to a laser-like focus, hitting your "Bullseye" becomes more likely. When you hit the center, your "sweet spot," then your execution of excellence will pull others in adjacent rings toward you. There are riches in the niches!

Why then do we try to market to the whole wide, wide world? We hope that by communicating randomly to everyone, the ones with whom we resonate will find us and come join our party. This big, broad-scale, generic marketing is costly and unless you are a national name with a product that is created for a giant section of the population, it isn't terribly effective.

Following is a diagram I use in my branding seminars to help people understand how to identify where they should focus their marketing efforts.

SELLING WITHOUT SLEAZE

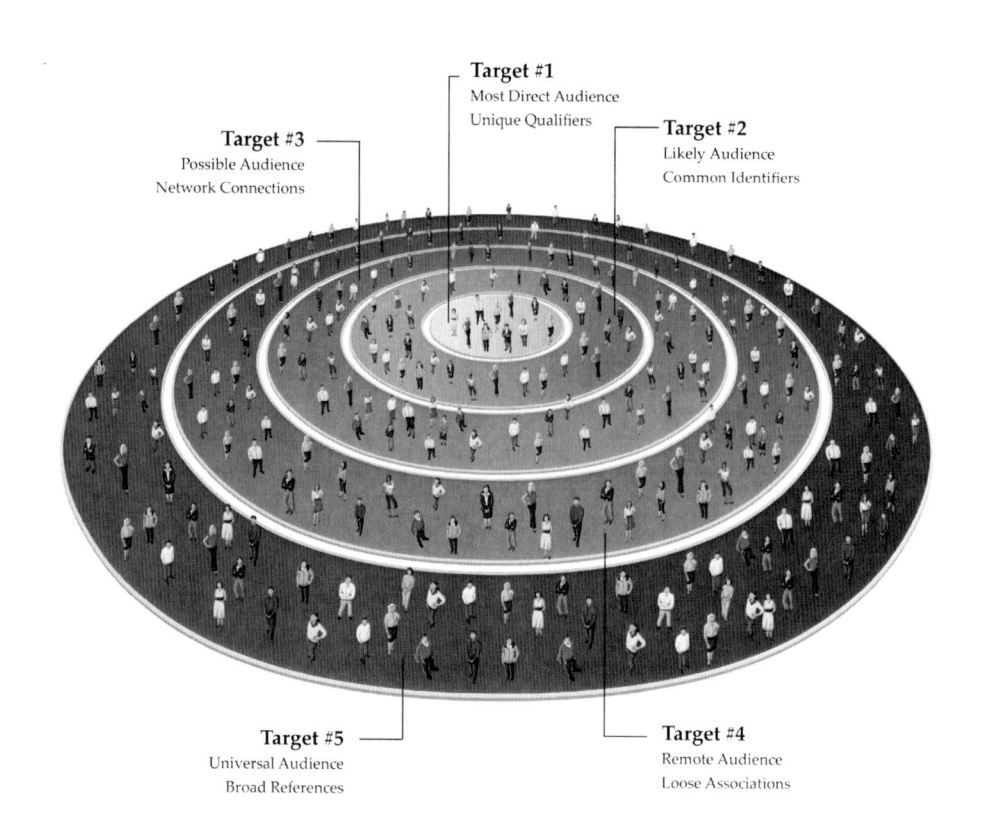

Target #1
Most Direct Audience
Unique Qualifiers

Target #2
Likely Audience
Common Identifiers

Target #3
Possible Audience
Network Connections

Target #4
Remote Audience
Loose Associations

Target #5
Universal Audience
Broad References

- **TARGET #1:** The very center of the bullseye is Target #1. This is your most direct audience. They will have unique qualifiers that make them distinctive from other people. Your own unique qualifiers will resonate closely with theirs—something about your experience, your view of the world, and how you function will grab their attention. They will feel like they have found their tribe when they find you! Focus your communication on reaching these people. Figure out where they are, what kind of books they are buying, what kind of seminars/classes they attend, what they have in common with each other. Nail that and you have just found your niche! The better you are at identifying this niche, the stronger your response from that niche will be.

- **TARGET #2:** In the ring just outside you'll find Target #2. This is also a likely audience for you. They will have some things in common with the people in Target #1. They may not feel as strongly about them, but there will be an intersection of interests, behaviors, and beliefs. If you have hit people in Target #1, they will communicate their excitement over finding you with people in Target #2 and bring them inside. Turn Target #1 people into fans and they will market you enthusiastically to Target #2 people without you spending any money or making any extraordinary efforts.

- **TARGET #3:** Adjacent to them is Target #3. This is your possible audience. These are people who have network connections to people in Target #1 and Target #2. They may be connected through a business or a professional network, they might have kids in the same school, or attend the same church. Maybe they share a hobby or are third cousins once removed. Their actual connections to each other are varied, diverse, and impossible for you to predict (which is why you can't market to it effectively). Just trust me that the world is connected. The stronger you resonate with people in the middle of your target market, the more likely it will be that people on an outer ring will come across you. It is like a pebble thrown into the water, the ripples go out, never in. The connection to someone in the center grants you access to an otherwise uninterested party and multiplication begins to take over. People begin to recognize you, even if they don't know too much about you. Momentum builds. Nothing attracts a crowd like a crowd—and people begin to connect to you in ways you could never have imagined possible. Are you seeing the trend?

- **TARGET #4:** Made up of a more remote audience, we find Target #4. These people have very loose associations with each other. The associations are broader, like being born in the same city, or affiliation with a political party, or fan of a certain sports team. There is still a common thread in them that can run through Targets #1, #2, and #3, but it is growing less and less specific. The target is broadening out. You can see why targeting this ring will not likely get you very many connections in the middle, your niche where people will be really excited about who you are and what you have to offer. Instead of trying to capture the attention of this broad audience and then identify the best prospects there, try working from the middle out. You have much stronger opportunity to connect there.

- **TARGET #5:** This is comprised of what I categorize as the universal audience. In Target #5 we have very broad connections. We live on earth … okay, maybe we have in common that we are Americans or British or Russian. We all had a mother. We have probably heard of Wal-Mart … my point is that our commonality is a broad, broad category of mankind. Trying to market to this universal group of people is folly. Even the big boys with multi-million dollar budgets know not to try this. (Well, a lot of churches try this … hoping to reach everybody, but it doesn't work for them either.) True, there is an occasional, random occurrence in which someone in this outside ring might be brought all the way into the center of your niche. The more common result is like a pebble tossed in the water, ripples go out not in.

IT ISN'T READY, FIRE, AIM

Don't fire before you aim. Don't aim before you are ready. Take time to identify your niche. Know everything you can about them and make yourself ready. Be prepared to encounter them in ways that are interesting to them. Know what problems they have and make sure your solution makes sense before you offer it. Aim well before you release your marketing arrows. Fire right at the center. The closer you get to the middle of your mark, the more opportunity for your influence to reverberate outward, increasing as it goes. Hit the outside ring and frustration and disappointment await you. The people you reach here are not interested in connecting with you. They do not have enough common passion in their pursuits to connect anyone else to you either.

4. ENDORSEMENTS AND TESTIMONIALS

When I book a hotel room or look up a restaurant online, I check out reviews written by total strangers. People I have never met inform me if the service was great or substandard ... and I totally believe them. In fact, they influence my decision. The same holds true for book and movie reviews. Even if you don't trust critics, chances are you listened to friends, family or co-workers who recommend you see, read, or steer clear. Angie's List has built a highly successful, national business around gathering customer reviews.

This is Biblical Marketing 101 in action: "Let another man praise you, and not your own mouth; a stranger and not your own lips."[7]

MARKETING 101

Endorsements and testimonials are powerful persuaders. When I first began working as a consultant, I went back to the people I had helped for free (before I began charging) and asked them to write me a short review or brief testimonial I could use to demonstrate how my service had benefited them. This is a pretty good strategy to build a client base in any business. You may provide some services for free in the beginning, asking only for honest feedback and the right to share that feedback with others.

The same strategy can apply to an author. When I coach people through the writing and publishing process, I have them name their dream endorsers. I ask, "If you could have anyone in the world endorse your book or write your Foreword, who would that be?" Then we ask. Sometimes we get a "no," but sometimes they write one for us!

When someone who is a recognized authority or personality endorses you or your work, you are in effect, borrowing their influence. Someone who doesn't know you recognizes them and trusts that if that person (whom they trust) endorsed you, you must be okay. Even if those who endorse you are your friends and have a circle no wider than your own, it has a positive effect. We like hearing what other people think and whether consciously or not, their opinions weigh in on our decisions.

This is what happens when others praise you. People trust what other people say about you above what you have to say about yourself.

Build testimonials and endorsements. It works. How do you get them? Ask.

5. SET THE RIGHT PRICE

This is who I am. This is what I have to offer. This is how much it costs …

This is one of the most difficult things to do. "How much do I charge?" has to be one of the hardest questions for people to answer. The Bible has some clear things to say on the subject of wages and setting prices:

- "In all labor there is profit."[8]

- "Do not muzzle an ox while it treads out the grain … the laborer is worthy of his wages."[9]

- "Do not have two differing weights in your bag—one heavy, one light. Do not have two differing measures in your house—one large, one small. You must have accurate and honest weights and measures, so that you may live

MARKETING 101

long in the land the Lord your God is giving you."[10]

- "The Lord detests dishonest scales, but accurate weights find favor with Him."[11]
- "The plans of the diligent lead to profit as surely as haste leads to poverty."[12]

… and these are just a few. The point I am driving home is that profit is godly. Jesus taught the parable of the talents, fully expecting that when He gives us something, He expects us to be fruitful and multiply it. He had little patience with the unprofitable steward.[13] God even told us He gave us the power to produce wealth to fulfill His covenant.[14] Earning money is not evil.

You must set a price that establishes profitability. If you are in business to sell a product, the price comes not only from the raw materials, but also from the overhead—labor, insurance, shipping, and a host of other expenses. These costs must be covered before one penny of the price of the product is considered profit.

If you are selling a service, you need to determine the fair market value of that service. Set your prices too low and you either attract the wrong client, or

SELLING WITHOUT SLEAZE

no clients at all. Set them too high and no one wants to work with you. Who else is doing something similar to what you are doing in the market where you function? What do they charge? How is your similar service distinctive? Does that allow you to charge more or does that make you the clear choice at the same price?

When I first began charging for my work as a consultant I was nervous about the price I set. I was afraid I wouldn't have any clients. I low-balled my prices. I had clients, but they were tiresome. They always wanted more and more services for the same money. They routinely asked for "gifts in kind" for their ministries, or tried to bargain my already too low prices down even lower. I constantly felt like I had to defend what I was charging and it was work, work, work all the time.

A wise mentor pushed me to double my fee. "Double? Are you crazy? I won't have any customers. The ones I have will leave and who will pay double?"

He was right. I doubled the price and the line to work with me got longer. The difficult clients who were always trying to get more out of me for less walked away. I engaged a new breed of customer who saw the value in what I did for them and were all too happy to write the checks.

MARKETING 101

That wasn't the last time I raised my fee, and each time I have done so it is because I have gotten better and better at what I do. I have serious, positive results I can point to. The line has not gotten any shorter, and the success of my business is growing because I am more careful to work with the right people. Having enough income allows me the freedom to turn income down when accepting means I would have to work with someone I don't fully believe in, or lend my anointing to a project I am not genuinely excited about.

In the meantime, I am now creating products for people at lower price points. These informational products provide know-how and expertise, but in a more "do-it-yourself" package. Using them does not require my personal consultation in order to experience some positive results. I can serve more people this way … and work less hours.

LET GENEROSITY FLOW

I am never without power to give, and neither are you. Just because you CAN command a high dollar as a speaker, coach, or consultant doesn't always mean you have to. You can give your products and services to whomever you will, anytime God leads. You can give discounts whenever you want, but it is hard to discount a service that hasn't been priced high enough in the first place. People need to understand the value of the product or service. When you give, it costs you something. You need to understand the value of what you are giving. When you have set the right prices for what you do, when you give it is by choice, with a cheerful heart, not under compulsion (or guilt trip or manipulation).[15] You sow seed in good ground when you recognize it.

My friend Lance Wallnau says, "There's nothing worse than a broke philanthropist." It's true. How can you give liberally if you don't have resources to direct? Having a profitable business allows you to put those profits to work behind any endeavor, mission, or ministry where you feel called.

I wish non-profit charities would see the value of creating for profit entities to function alongside them. The for profit business does not even have to be in a related field, but having profitable businesses aligned with you can be beneficial. Business owners who share your values and see the bigger picture of what you feel called to accomplish allows you the freedom to put some of those business profits to work for the work of the ministry!

I know when I give freely, I grow richer. When I withhold my hand, I suffer lack.[16] I know it is God who makes my name great, and that I am blessed to be a blessing.[17] I know that a generous man prospers, and every time I water others, I am refreshed.[18]

Being brilliant in business lets me do more for the kingdom than ever before. Keep your scales just. Walk in wisdom and be profitable!

6. MECHANIZE TO MONETIZE

This is who I am. This is what I have to offer. This is how much it costs. This is how you get it …

Now that someone has found you and they are excited about what you have to offer and find it valuable enough to buy it, how do they obtain it? How do they purchase? How can they work with you? Mechanizing your process will allow more people to engage.

Marketing allows you the opportunity to be creative and resourceful. No matter how seasoned you are or how much experience you have, all marketing has a little bit of trial and error in the mix. You have to discover what works for you. What reaches your target audience and resonates with them?

SELLING WITHOUT SLEAZE

- **HAVE A SOLID WEB PAGE**

    This sounds pretty basic, and it is. Surprisingly, I still meet people every day who want to connect with the world, but don't have a website. Or they have a website, but it is so poorly crafted visitors bounce before they browse.

    Your site should clearly communicate what it is you do and how it will benefit them from the opening of the home page. A shot of your logo, photo, and "Welcome" is pretty generic. As a visitor I am thinking, "What's your thing? Why should I stay and browse? You have only seconds to capture my attention or I move on." Does your website have a "hook" that grabs their notice? Is there any bait on that hook? Is it the right bait?

    Spend some time developing your content. Is there anything a visitor can learn that will benefit or interest them without buying something from you? Are you enough of an expert that you have free content available that is valuable?

    Creating an "opt in" can be a good strategy to help build your audience and keep people interested and engaged with you. An "opt in" is something of value you offer for free in exchange for a site visitor's name and email address. This might be an ebook or an audio download. It could be a white paper or a check list. When I speak, I generally provide notes for people to follow along and fill in the blanks. I always offer to send them a copy with all the blanks filled in if they want to visit my website and leave me their information. This yields great results. They have come by choice to receive something from me and now have the opportunity to stay connected for a longer conversation.

- **REMOVE BARRIERS TO ENTRY**

I have found that the easier it is to conduct business with you, the more likely people will be to give it a try. I seek to remove as many barriers to entry as I can. I want the path to be easy to follow and clear to navigate. I don't want them to have to click two buttons if they can do it by clicking one.

For people who speak professionally, I encourage an "INVITE" tab on your web page. This tab should include a downloadable press kit which allows someone access to all the information they need from you without even having to make a phone call. They should be able to access your bio, high resolution photographs, endorsements, products or resources you offer all before they even contact you. Many people want to know all the logistics before they reach out. If they can't find them, they sometimes pass you over even if you were exactly who they needed. Remove barriers to entry.

Whether or not you want your pricing available on your website is up to you. In a store for products, you obviously have to list your prices. If you have standard coaching packages, that should also be clearly communicated. Sometimes prices are not listed for higher end professional consulting services, or when a customized quote is required. In these situations, it is not practical to list pricing. But even under these circumstances, people should be able to request more information or initiate a quote electronically.

Many people do not like making a phone call. They want to click a button, make their inquiry, and have an email reply with the information. You need to have a clear package available to send so they can find out what they want to know. If having to make a phone call is a barrier to initiating business with you … remove the barrier.

Visit your website objectively through the eyes of a brand new browser. Click through all the pages. Buy something from your own store. Is the experience pleasant or frustrating? Was it easy to navigate?

MARKETING 101

- ## USE MORE THAN ONE CHANNEL

    Having a website is an absolute must, but there are lots of other platforms out there to help you be a wise steward of your influence. Facebook, Twitter, Pinterest, Google+, LinkedIn ... there are more channels out there than you could possibly manage well. I recommend you choose a few you can stick with and work regularly, or hire someone who is gifted in this arena and put them to work for you.

    When I work with authors, I highly encourage them to get active on Amazon and utilize CreateSpace and Kindle as well as have books available on their own sites. You can be a member of Goodreads.com, AuthorsDen.com, and dozens of other author-friendly sites to help broaden your territory. If you aren't T.D. Jakes or John Maxwell and have a name that will sell books regardless of the content, it is a little harder to get into brick and mortar bookstores, but it isn't impossible. Set your sights for where you want to go, then run in that direction!

- ## KEEP THINKING OUTSIDE THE BOX

    The most successful people I know are not "One Hit Wonders." They don't just create one opportunity and count on that for the next ten years. Keep challenging yourself to think beyond where you are today and reach for new things. Continue to refine your craft, revisit products and services you have created—improve, expand, and grow. You buy new clothes from time to time and get a haircut. Why? Because seasons change and you have to tend to your appearance unless you want to grow shabby. Your brand image requires the same kind of attention. The major things don't change, but you need to update your appearance occasionally. You need to make sure the things you offer are "in style" ... relevant for a current, changing audience.

We have just covered some of the basics of marketing. Hopefully you are feeling a little more comfortable with the idea of offering yourself to the world. Marketing yourself does not mean there is something prideful or ugly inside of you. It doesn't have to be self-aggrandizing. It doesn't have to be slick. It shouldn't be accidental either. It should be done on purpose—with intentionality and excellence.

Marketing yourself means you understand there is something worthwhile inside of you that other people need to be able to connect to. Not sharing what you have is selfish, it may even be the result of false humility. As surely as I believe branding is intentionally coming into agreement with God's identity in you, I believe marketing is demonstrating honor for His assignment to you. When

MARKETING 101

you confidently own who you are and what you do, you are creating opportunities to be the best steward possible of the influence, anointing, and expertise He has placed inside you. Be a wise and profitable steward.

You can market who you are and what you have to offer without manipulating people. You can market successfully without compromising your moral code or values system.

Now that we have that settled, let's take a step back and get a broader perspective.

ENDNOTES:

1. Colossians 3:23.
2. Matthew 21:12.
3. Proverbs 22:1.
4. 2 Corinthians 3:15-18.
5. Daniel 3.
6. John 21:6.
7. Proverbs 27:2.
8. Proverbs 14:23.
9. 1 Timothy 5:18.
10. Deuteronomy 25:13-15, NIV.
11. Proverbs 11:1, NIV.
12. Proverbs 21:5, NIV.
13. Matthew 25:14-30.
14. Deuteronomy 8:18.
15. 2 Corinthians 9:7.
16. Proverbs 11:24.
17. Genesis 12:2.
18. Proverbs 11:25.

SELLING WITHOUT SLEAZE

CHAPTER FOUR

THE BIGGER PICTURE

I love business. I love meeting confident people who are really good at what they do. I love finding quality products and appreciate distinctive service. I am passionate about helping people figure out what they are best at and love to do most. I challenge them to own that completely. I love guiding people to discover what they have that is valuable and assist them in connecting to people who want what they've got.

I love it when someone who has struggled with wanting to make a difference in the world, influence the culture, and serve God discovers this doesn't necessarily mean they need to work full time for a church or ministry. It doesn't mean they can't be brilliant at what they do or be successful at it. When someone gets it that their work can be worship—thoroughly consecrated to the Lord on Wall Street or Main Street, I do a backflip!

Aristotle said, "Other things being equal, human beings enjoy the exercise of their realized capacities (their innate or trained abilities), and this enjoyment increases the more the capacity is realized ..." It's true. The better you get at what you are naturally wired to do, the more fun it is to do it.

Here's the thing about destiny: it is never just about you. There is a bigger picture. There is a possibility that when you discover your purpose and get excited about fufilling your destiny you can become self-centric, self-pleasing, and self-serving. This is the inherent danger of self-discovery (and of personal branding). It can lead to becoming so in tune with your own preferences, your own temperament, strengths, and gifts that you become a fantastic tornado of self. You can get so wrapped up in being who you are, spinning around impressively, that you don't notice you are destroying the habitation of others along the way.

Your destiny is wrapped in your identity. How you were created is a clue to why you were created. Design reveals purpose. A crystal wine glass was created to hold a superb vintage, meant to be comfortable next to fine china and silver. Can it be used to hold milk

THE BIGGER PICTURE

or fruit juice? Yes. Could it be a vase for flowers? Yes. If shipwrecked on an island with survival on the line and the only vessel available, could it be used as a scoop or shovel? Yes. The wine glass can be functional in many roles, but other uses are not its highest and best purpose. In fact, the further it gets away from what it was designed for, the greater the potential it will become damaged or broken and no longer able to fulfill the destiny for which it was created.

The same holds true for us. The further we get from our destiny, the less fulfilled we are, even if our functionality remains. Knowing who we are, how we are wired, what we are best at, and what we love to do most helps us discover what we are called to do. It helps us step into our destiny. But, our destiny is not independent of other people. Like a beautiful, brightly colored, interesting ceramic tile placed carefully in a mosaic, we were meant to be part of a bigger picture.

Who we are is meant to flow effortlessly next to someone else. Our shapes, highlights, and shadows bring out the beauty in others. We are a unique and important piece of a whole—we are not the whole. Knowing who we are and where we fit is extremely valuable. Owning our bright colors and odd shapes allows us to love our placement and relax about things we are not.

SELLING WITHOUT SLEAZE

Learning about yourself does not mean you have to become self-centered. It can be used to heighten your awareness and become more intentional about where you direct your efforts and your resources.

I wrote this book because I constantly encounter people who are struggling with the idea of promoting themselves or things they have created. It feels too much like pride. It feels too self-serving. I so appreciate where they are coming from. I respect the struggle. I have wrestled it too.

If you have struggled with the idea of making money or being successful, please remember that if you commit your works to the Lord, your plans will succeed.[1]

There is an abundance of guidance available to you to keep your way pure. Being successful is a good thing! A man of integrity can expect all that he does to prosper.[2] In all labor there is profit.[3] If you work, there should be reward. There should be good return on your investments. "When he returned … he ordered these servants to whom he had given the money to be called to him, that he might know what they had gained by doing business."[4]

If you know you have something good to share, please don't shrink back from marketing this to other people because you have seen too many sleazy salesman and were turned off. "And just as you want men to do to you, you also do to them likewise."[5] You can market to others

THE BIGGER PICTURE

in the same way you would want to be marketed to. Sell without sleaze. Tell people who you are, what you have to offer, what it costs, and how to get it.

ENDNOTES :

1. Proverbs 16:3.
2. Psalm 1:1-3.
3. Proverbs 14:23.
4. Luke 19:15, ESV.
5. Luke 6:31.

SELLING WITHOUT SLEAZE

Wendy K. Walters
Live on Purpose

Wendy K. Walters has a gift for identifying what makes a person unique and bringing that to the forefront. Like few others, she can guide you through the maze of distinctions that make you stand out—looking better and sharper, maximizing your originality. As a consultant she has helped launch many people's dreams, translating their ideas into profitable businesses.

Author of *Marketing Your Mind*; *Postworthy—Words to Encourage and Inspire*; and *Intentionality—Live on Purpose!* Wendy has also developed a powerful *Brand Profile* that recognizes core competencies, pinpoints core values, identifies the problems you are uniquely gifted to solve, helps target your niche market, and develop your signature brand.

Wendy coaches people through the process of developing intellectual property and has the resources available to bring those ideas across the finish line into tangible reality—creating products and platforms for services.

She speaks at conferences and business events, activating and empowering people to declare their dreams, identify with their passion, and create strategic action plans. Wendy points others confidently toward their destiny and encourages them to walk each day with intentionality—living with purpose, on purpose! She finds no greater joy than seeing others released into their potential and living 100% fully alive.

www.wendykwalters.com

MARKETING YOUR MIND is written in three parts:

- Brand Yourself
- Write Your Book
- Market Your Ideas

Drawing from her experience both as a branding consultant and as a partner in Palm Tree Productions, Wendy offers you a practical, simple guide to developing your intellectual property and turning your ideas into marketable products and processes.

A rounded arrow pierces no target! Mediocrity is the hallmark of the well-rounded individual. Becoming a "jack of all trades, but master of none" is the result when strengths and passion are not consciously cultivated.

You must participate in the design of your own future. **INTENTIONALITY** will help you sharpen your arrow and take aim at a specific target. Identify your passion and discover all that makes you unique, then focus your choices, your resources, and your energy on developing mastery in your field.

Stop being swept along by life's current. Take the helm of your destiny and step into your unlimited future. Begin to live fully engaged, fully alive—live with purpose … on purpose!

Available at:

w w w . w e n d y k w a l t e r s . c o m

Speaker | Author | Consultant

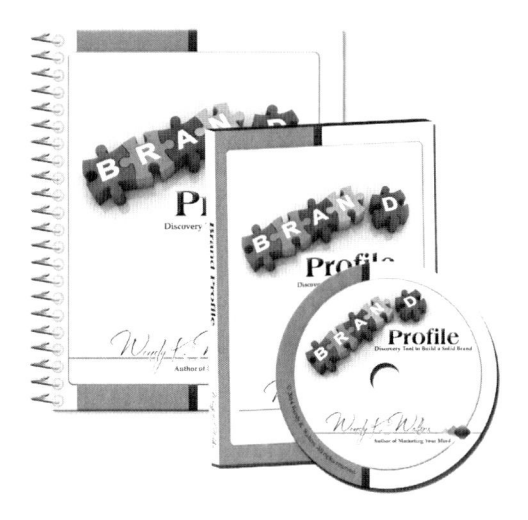

The **BRAND PROFILE** is an assessment tool created to take you through a process of discovery to identify your "unique factor" and pull out your core competencies, core values, developed skill sets, and areas of mastery. It helps evaluate your intellectual property to target your market and develop a signature brand. Wendy uses this tool with her clients and has now made it available for personal use.

BONUS: Included with the **BRAND PROFILE** is a section geared toward "info-preneurs"—those who are focused on speaking professionally, coaching, and consulting.

Available at:

www.wendykwalters.com

Speaker | Author | Consultant

WRITE A REVIEW

1. Go to amazon.com.
2. Search for *Selling Without Sleaze* by Wendy K. Walters.
3. Scroll all the way to the bottom and click on the button, **"Write a Customer Review."**
4. Rate the book (out of 5 stars) and write your review.
5. Submit.

Note: You do not have to purchase the book on amazon to leave a review. Anyone with an amazon account is eligible to write a review for any book they have read.

Thank You!